113758 EN
Weight

Sullivan, Navin
ATOS BL 6.8
Points: 1.0   MG

Measure Up!

WEIGHT

Navin Sullivan

mc **Marshall Cavendish**
Benchmark
New York

Marshall Cavendish Benchmark
99 White Plains Road
Tarrytown, New York 10591
www.marshallcavendish.us

All Web sites were available and accurate when this book was sent to press.

Library of Congress Cataloging-in-Publication Data

Sullivan, Navin.
    Weight / Navin Sullivan.
        p. cm. — (Measure up!)
    Summary: "Discusses weight, the science behind measuring weight, and the different devices used to measure
weight"—Provided by publisher.
    Includes bibliographical references and index.
    ISBN-13: 978-0-7614-2324-9
    ISBN-10: 0-7614-2324-9
    1. Weight (Physics)—Measurement—Juvenile literature. I. Title.
QC90.6.S86 2006
530.8'1—dc22
2006020816

Editor: Karen Ang
Editorial Director: Michelle Bisson
Art Director: Anahid Hamparian
Series Designer: Alex Ferrari

Photo Research by Iain Morrison

Cover: Brand X/SuperStock

The photographs in this book are used by permission and through the courtesy of: *Alamy:* Comstock Images, 1; Mary
Evans Picture Library, 7; Ashley Cooper, 33. *Art Resource, Inc.:* Werner Forman, 12. *Corbis:* Gianni Dagli Orti, 14;
Bettmann, 15; Andrew Brookes, 18; Albrecht G. Schaefer, 30. *The Image Works:* SSPL, 20, 36, 38; Ann Ronan Picture
Library/HIP, 21, 29; Rachel Epstein, 28; David Lassmann/Syracuse Newspapers, 42. *Photo Researchers, Inc.:* David A
Hardy, 9; NASA, 11; Adam Hart-Davis, 22; Jean-Loup Charmet, 23; Ton Kinsbergen, 24; Perennou Nuridsany, 32;
Roger Harris, 34; Scott Camazine, 39; Mauro Fermariello, 41. *Science Photo Library:* Charles D. Winters, 26.
SuperStock: Age Fotostock, 4, 17.

Printed in China
1 3 5 6 4 2

Contents

Gravity is the force that acts upon all matter on Earth. Gravity pulls these grains of sand through the neck of the hourglass.

CHAPTER ONE
What Is Weight?

Lift a rubber ball or one of your favorite sneakers. Let go of it and what happens? It drops to the floor. But why does it fall? Earth is pulling on it, and this pull is called **gravity.** Earth's gravity prevents the object from floating upward. It also holds you safely on the ground. Gravity even pulls on the Moon and keeps it going around Earth instead of heading off into outer space.

Every object pulls on other objects. In most cases, this gravitational pull is a very weak force—most of the time you do not even notice it. But the force of the pull is affected by **mass.** Mass is the amount of matter something has. An object with more mass will have a stronger gravitational pull than an object with less mass. For example, a grain of dust has a gravitational pull. But the grain's mass is so small that we do not notice its pull on us. Earth has an incredibly large mass, so we can feel the planet's gravity as a strong pull. Just as Earth's gravity pulls on you, your gravity pulls on Earth. But your pull is much weaker because the planet is much bigger than you.

Mass and weight are not the same thing, but they are closely related. How much you weigh depends on how much mass you have, which then affects the level of gravitational force pulling on you. Simply put, weight is the amount of gravitational pull on an object.

THE PLANETS

Whirling clouds of gas in galaxies gradually clump together to form stars. Sometimes the rings of gas around the stars clump together to form planets. Gravity is the force that pulls the gases together.

The Moon is much smaller than Earth, so its gravity is only one-sixth the strength of Earth's gravity. If you were on the Moon you would have the same mass as you do on Earth, but you would only weigh one-sixth as much. Your weight is reduced because of the Moon's weaker gravitational pull. When American astronaut Neil Armstrong walked on the Moon in 1969, his steps became large bounds. This is because his muscles were built for walking on Earth with its stronger gravitational pull. However, on Jupiter, which has a gravity 2.4 times stronger than Earth's gravity, you would not even be able to lift a foot!

THE LAW OF GRAVITY

In 1687, British scientist Sir Isaac Newton formulated the Law of Gravity. Newton realized that all matter has a gravitational force. He calculated the effects of gravity and how it works throughout the universe.

He showed that how much one object pulls on another depends on three things: the gravitational forces between the objects, the masses of the objects, and the distance between the objects.

When he was a young man, Isaac Newton realized that the force which pulled an apple to the ground also pulled the Moon toward Earth. He was even able to calculate mathematically the orbit of the Moon.

GRAVITY AND DISTANCE

An object's gravitational pull surrounds the object. But as distance from the object increases, the strength of the gravitational force decreases. For example, the pull of Earth's gravity radiates outward from Earth's center. The farther you are from that center, the weaker Earth's pull on you will be.

The surface of Earth is about 4,000 miles from the planet's center. Yet the planet's gravitational pull on you is still strong enough to keep you from floating away. Just think of how strong the pull would be if you were very close to the center!

Imagine you are traveling to the Moon. From the moment of lift-off Earth's pull on you starts decreasing. As you climb higher, heading toward space, the pull of the Moon starts affecting you. At a certain point, the Moon's pull will equal Earth's pull on you. When you reach that point you will be weightless. After that, the pull of the Moon is greater than Earth's, and you begin to fall toward the Moon.

Even when you are on the Moon, Earth's gravity will be pulling on you, but you will not notice it. Because you are so far away, Earth's pull will only be 1/3,600 of what it is on Earth's surface. The Moon's pull on you will be much stronger.

SATELLITES

Newton also thought about how objects can travel far in spite of gravity. Newton imagined that he fired a ball from a cannon at the top of a mountain. The force of the cannon would overcome gravity to send the ball about a mile or so. Then gravity would make the ball fall. If the cannon were more powerful, the ball would go farther, but would still eventually fall. What if the ball were fired from a super-cannon? If the ball traveled with a force that was equal to the force of gravity pulling the ball down, the two forces would act together on the ball. This would make the ball circle around Earth. Assuming there was no air pushing against it to slow it down, the ball would keep going around forever! This is the basic concept behind how satellites work. Using the same reasoning, Newton also calculated how Earth's gravity keeps the Moon going around Earth and how the Sun's gravity keeps Earth orbiting the Sun.

Newton had worked out mathematically how an artificial satellite could exist, but in 1686 he could not possibly make one. That occurred hundreds of years later, in 1957, when The Soviet Union put the first artificial satellite—*Sputnik 1*—into orbit.

This illustration shows the Soviet satellite *Sputnik 1* orbiting Earth. The satellite had four antennas that sent information back to the scientists on Earth.

WEIGHING NOTHING

People do not need to travel all the way to the Moon to be weightless. Being in orbit around Earth will work just as well. When a space station or space shuttle orbits the planet, the crew inside does not feel Earth's gravity. This is because the gravitational pull is canceled out by the speed of the orbiting object. This makes everything inside the station or shuttle weightless.

Being in a weightless environment has strange results. For instance, you cannot pour a drink into your mouth because the drink has no weight. The liquid would just float away. In order to drink, you would have to squeeze the fluid into your mouth instead. If you get up quickly, you may soar across the cabin of the space station because gravity does not pull you down. So your movements have to be smaller and more controlled. But weightlessness also has very good benefits. If something needs to be repaired outside the station, the weightlessness allows an astronaut to move heavy metal parts that might need to be bolted to the station.

Because astronauts are weightless in space, they do not need to use a lot of strength to move around. As a result, their muscles and bones may become weak, which can lead to health problems. Special exercises help the astronauts keep their muscles and bones fit and strong.

This wall painting from an Egyptian tomb shows metalworkers using a balance to weigh gold.

CHAPTER TWO

Measuring Weight

THE BALANCE

To weigh something actually means that we are comparing the object's weight with another weight that has already been measured. To measure weight nearly 3,500 years ago, Ancient Egyptians used a balance arm suspended at its center. A pan at one end of the arm held what they were weighing. They hung known weights at the other end of the arm until the arm was **horizontal.** When the arm was horizontal, they knew that the weight of the object equaled the amount of known weights.

THE SEE-SAW

The see-saw is a type of balance. It is a long plank set upon a central balancing point, which is called a **pivot.** Suppose you and a friend sit at opposite ends of the plank. If you weigh more, your end of the see-saw will go down. If you weigh less, your end will go up, while your friend's end will go down. How can you get the see-saw to level out? The see-saw works by combining the effect of someone's weight and where he or she sits on the plank. The half of the plank that you are sitting on can be called the arm. When you sit on a see-saw, where you

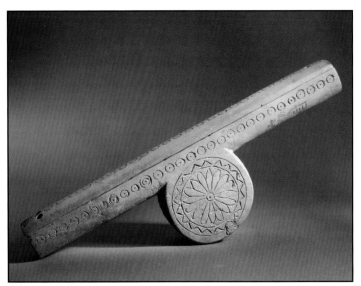

Ancient Egyptians used this wooden balance to compare the weights of different objects.

sit on the arm increases the effect of your weight. This means that you are using the arm as a **lever**, to increase the effect of your weight.

You can adjust the length of the arm by moving away from or toward the pivot. If you sit at the far end of the plank, you are using the full length of the arm, and will get the maximum effect of your weight. Decreasing the length of the arm lessens the effect of your weight. If you are heavier, you can balance your friend on the other end of the see-saw by moving closer to the pivot. This will decrease the length of the arm and decrease the effect of your weight. If you are lighter, you need a longer part of the arm and your friend will need a shorter part.

THE STEELYARD

Two or three centuries after the first Ancient Egyptian balance, the Ancient Romans invented the steelyard. Like the Ancient Egyptian balance, it hung from a chain. However, it did not require many weights.

Instead, the Romans used the principle of the lever to alter the effect of a single measuring weight.

One arm of the steelyard was longer than the other. A standard metal weight hung from the long arm. The shorter arm had a fixed hook or pan to hold the goods being weighed. To alter the effect of the standard weight, the merchant slid the weight along the arm. To balance heavy products, he slid the weight toward the end of the arm. For something lighter, he moved it closer to the center. Notches along the arm showed different balancing points. When the steelyard was

A trader and a Native American hunter use a steelyard to weigh furs the hunter has collected. Steelyards sometimes had a pan at one end or a hook to hang objects being weighed.

horizontal and balanced, the merchant knew the weight of the products. Today, the steelyard is still used in some parts of southern Europe.

THE SPRING SCALE

If you squeeze or compress a spring to a shorter length and then let it go, it springs back to its original length. Stretch it, then release it, and again it returns to its usual length. In 1676 an English scientist, Robert Hooke, experimented with steel springs. He hung one up and attached a weighing pan to the bottom of the spring.

When he put a weight into the pan, the spring was stretched. If he put a heavier weight into the pan, the spring was stretched farther. Hooke discovered that the amount by which the spring was stretched varied depending upon the object being weighed. The object's weight could be calculated by measuring the spring compression. His work led to the spring scale, first made in 1694.

Your bathroom scales work on the same principle. Stand on the platform and you compress a spring. The scale registers the compression as your weight. Some scales electronically convert the compression into a digital display. Either way, you are measuring your weight with a spring.

ELECTRONIC SCALES

Electronic scales are used when lighter objects are weighed. These scales are usually more sensitive than spring scales or balances, and can measure weight in smaller fractions. For example, a pharmacy has electronic scales for weighing tiny pills. The scales use the force from a magnet to counter the weight of the pills. When you use a magnet to pick up thumb tacks, the magnetic force is countering—or working against—the weight of the tacks. The magnets in an electronic scale work in a similar manner.

The scales have the weighing pan sitting on a coil of wire. The coil is held at a specific level by a magnetic force. This force comes from an **electromagnet** surrounding the coil. The electromagnet contains metal that is only magnetized when an electric current is passed through the coil. As the pan is filled with objects to be weighed, it pushes the coil down. The coil eventually interrupts a beam of light that is crossing its path. This then triggers a current to flow in the coil around the electromagnet, sending out magnetic force. This force lifts the coil to its original position. The amount of current needed to do this indicates the weight of the object in the pan. The amount of current is usually converted and displayed as a weight.

Electronic scales are used to measure very light objects. Post offices use electronic scales to weigh letters and packages.

Standardized metal weights are used to compare the weights of different objects. The standard weights can be made from brass, silver, or other types of metals.

CHAPTER THREE

Units of Weight

TRADITIONAL WEIGHTS

The first weights were made of stone but, bronze and brass were later used. Different sizes were chosen to make weights as heavy or light as needed. Basic units of weight in ancient times were usually based on a standard number of seeds from particular plants.

One of the earliest weights was the **shekel**. This was first devised by the Ancient Babylonians. These Babylonians lived in Mesopotamia, which is now a part of present-day Iraq. The shekel was a very small weight—only about 1/4 of the ounce we use today. A heavier weight was the *mina*, which equaled about 50 shekels. The mina was about the weight of our pound. The *talent* was even heavier, weighing about 60 minas.

The Ancient Romans chose another weight as their standard. They called it the *libra*, which equaled about 3/4 of today's pound. (We abbreviate pound as lb. today because lb. stands for libra.) The Romans then divided the libra into various fractions, and named them all. A useful fraction was 1/12 libra, called the *uncia*. (Uncia means one-twelfth in Latin.) In English, libra became *pound* and uncia became *ounce*. For a long while afterward, apothecaries (who were similar to modern-day pharmacists) had their own measures, which included the ounce that was equal to 1/12 pound. (Today, the ordinary ounce is equal to 1/16 pound.)

The Roman libra was used all over Europe. Then it was taken by the Spanish to South America. There its measure increased about 40 percent. This might have occurred because the plant seeds used in South America as the standard were heavier than the European seeds. Today, the U.S. pound still weighs about 40 percent more than the Roman libra.

The Roman libra was also the name of a unit of money. (Similarly, the British use pound today for both weight and money.) In the same way, the Babylonian shekel was used by the ancient Hebrews both as a unit of weight and as a unit of money. In modern Israel, the shekel is still the country's official currency.

Weights used by English settlers who traveled to the United States were copied from England. Unfortunately, English measures

These bronze uncia weights were used by the Romans more than one thousand years ago.

This engraving from the fifteenth century shows how standard weights were often tested for accuracy. If they did not weigh the correct amounts, the weights were burned or destroyed.

The metal measuring cups (front row) and metal weights (back row) were used by the English in the sixteenth century.

varied from one part of England to another, so all over the United States, different measures were being used. For instance, a bushel of oats in Connecticut weighed 28 pounds, while in New Jersey it weighed 32 pounds. Later, the confusion was increased by Dutch, French, and Spanish settlers who brought their own measures.

To end the confusion of different traditional measures, John Quincy Adams in 1821 proposed that the United States adopt the metric system. This had been devised by the French after the French

Revolution of 1790. Adams believed that the metric system would avoid confusion and lead to an era of peace and goodwill. However, he warned that the American people would probably prefer to stick to traditional measures for everyday use. In 1893, the United States decided to officially adopt the metric system.

METRIC WEIGHTS

The French devised the metric system after the French Revolution. First, they chose a standard unit of length—the meter. They defined this as 1/40,000,000 of Earth's **circumference** (the distance around Earth). In 1799 they figured out how to measure Earth's circumference and were then able to establish the meter. The French then used the meter to define weight.

They divided the meter into one hundred centimeters (*centi* meaning one

This French illustrations shows how the metric system was used for measuring liquids (1), balancing fine measurements (2), measuring cloth (3), checking the height of a wall (4), weighing currency (5), and measuring a bundle of cut wood (6).

hundred). They took a cubic centimeter of freezing pure water and weighed it at **sea level.** (A cubic centimeter is a cube with sides that measure 1 centimeter each.) The French measured this at sea level because they knew that the cubic centimeter would weigh different amounts at different altitudes, or heights. The weight of the cubic centimeter of water at sea level was defined as 1 gram. They then defined the kilogram as 1,000 grams and made that their basic standard of weight. (*Kilo* comes from the Greek word for thousand.)

These brass weights are used to balance objects placed in a weighing pan.

In 1890, the French shipped a gift-wrapped bar weighing exactly 1 kilogram to United States President Benjamin Harrison. The bar was made of a mixture of two metals, platinum and iridium. (Today, the bar is held by the National Institute of Standards and Technology.)

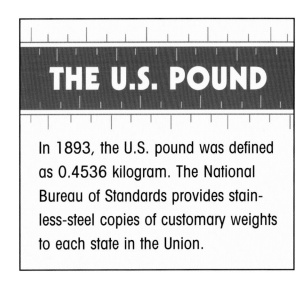

THE U.S. POUND

In 1893, the U.S. pound was defined as 0.4536 kilogram. The National Bureau of Standards provides stainless-steel copies of customary weights to each state in the Union.

Ever since then, the kilogram has been the official United States benchmark of mass. Scientists and engineers in the United States have adopted the metric system of weights and other measures.

Though the metric system may be the official measurement standard, most Americans use traditional or customary units—such as the pound or ounce. In most other countries, however, the metric system is used for everyday life.

This experiment shows how liquid mercury, copper, and water have different densities. The mercury is at the bottom of the tube because it is the most dense. The copper balls are less dense, so they float above the mercury. Water is less dense than both copper and mercury, so it rests on top of the copper balls.

CHAPTER FOUR

Density

The amount of space that an object occupies is called its **volume.**
This space can be measured by distance—in cubic feet—or by liquid
volume—in pints or gallons. Some objects weigh more than others
even when they have the same volume. For example, an aluminum
cooking pan is lighter than an iron pan of the same size because iron is
a heavier metal. A metal ruler weighs more than a plastic one. A pint
of water weighs less than a pint of cooking oil. When two objects have
the same volume, but have different weights, the objects are said to
have different densities. An object's density is its weight divided by its
volume. Density can be measured in pounds per cubic foot or kilograms per liter.

Density = Weight ÷ Volume

When you put an object into a container of liquid—water, for
instance—the liquid will usually rise. This is called **displacement.**
The object is displacing a specific amount of water from the container. The
amount of water that is displaced is equal to the volume of the object.
For example, if an object displaces 3 cubic feet of water, the volume of
that object is 3 cubic feet.

If two objects of the same weight displace different volumes, then
their densities are different. Displacement gives us a way to compare

A rock's volume can be determined using displacement. Before the rock is put inside the measuring cup (left) the water fills 300 milliliters (300 mL) of the cup. Once the rock is placed inside (right), the water rises to 400 mL. This means that 100 mL of water was displaced by the rock, which shows that the rock's volume is 100 mL.

densities. The man who first realized this was Archimedes, a mathematician and inventor who lived in Sicily, then a colony of Ancient Greece.

Around 200 BCE, Hiero became the new ruler of Syracuse, a city in Sicily. To celebrate, he wanted a crown of pure gold placed in a temple. He appointed a craftsman to make it and gave the craftsman the exact amount of gold to use. When the crown arrived it looked perfect and it weighed the same amount as the gold. However, Hiero suspected that the crown might be gold mixed with cheaper silver. How could he find out?

Hiero turned to Archimedes for help. Archimedes thought about the problem while going to the public bathhouse. Silver is lighter than gold, so a mixture of silver and gold would be less dense (or have a lower density) than pure gold. In order for the silver-and-gold crown to weigh as much as a pure gold crown, the silver-and-gold crown's volume must be greater. But how could Archimedes check the crown's volume?

A German illustration from the sixteenth century shows Archimedes in a bathtub, where he discovered the principle of displacement. This enabled him to demonstrate that Hiero's gold crown was fake. When he realized this, he shouted "*Eureka!*" which is Greek for "I have found it!"

Archimedes stepped into a full tub of water and slowly sat down.

Water then started overflowing from the tub because he was displacing some of the water. The deeper he sank into the tub, the more the water overflowed. In a flash, the answer came to him. He could measure the crown's volume by how much water it displaced. Because a crown made of silver and gold would have a larger volume, it would displace more water than a crown of pure gold.

Archimedes made two objects that weighed the same as the crown. One was of pure silver and the other was made of pure gold. He checked how much water each object displaced. Pure gold displaced less water than pure silver. Archimedes compared their displacements with that of Hiero's crown. Compared to pure gold of the same weight, the crown displaced more water. The crown also displaced less water than pure silver of the same weight. This proved that, as Hiero had suspected, the crown was a mixture of gold and silver. Hiero had been swindled! Archimedes's discovery was later used to check whether coins were made of pure metal or a cheaper mixture of metals.

FLOTATION

An object will float on water if its density is less than the density of water. Wood has a lot of air in it and ice is less dense than water. Drop a piece of wood in water and it will displace a little bit of water, but less than the amount of its own volume. The surrounding water holds up the wood, making it float.

Ice is less dense than water. That is why ice—in nature or in your drinking glass—floats.

Solid iron is much denser than water, so a piece of solid iron put into water drops to the bottom of the container. But how do big iron ships float? The iron structure of the ship encloses a lot of air. Together, the iron and air are less dense than solid iron. They are also less dense than water, so the ship will float.

BUOYANCY

A floating ship displaces water. The amount of water that it displaces depends on the density of the water. (Remember, if an object is less dense than water it will float.) Salt water is denser than fresh water, so a ship displaces less water in the ocean than it does in the fresh waters of the Great Lakes. We say that salt water is more buoyant and allows the ship to float more easily. As a result, a ship can carry a greater load in salt water than in fresh water.

Temperature also affects the buoyancy of water. Warm water is less dense than cold water. A ship traveling in the warm waters along the Florida coast floats lower than it would in the colder waters of Newfoundland, Canada.

PLIMSOLL LINES

Merchant ships have lines—called Plimsoll Lines—on the outside of the ship. These lines show how much cargo the ship can hold while floating safely in different waters. When a ship is being loaded in a harbor, it can be loaded until the appropriate line reaches the surface of the water.

COMPARING THE DENSITIES OF LIQUIDS

Materials you will need:

A clear measuring cup (at least 2 pints or 1 quart)

3/4 cup of a heavy oil, such as corn oil

3/4 cup of a light oil, such as sunflower oil

3/4 cup of water colored with food coloring

Objects of different densities: a grape, an eraser, and a wedge of potato.

Pour the heavy oil into the measuring cup. Then pour the lighter oil and then the colored water.

The three liquids should make different bands in the cylinder because they have different densities.

Now put in the different objects. Why does each object sink to a different level? *(Answer appears on page 47.)*

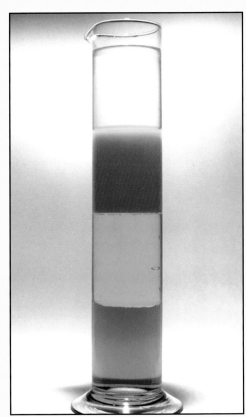

Liquids with different densities will float above one another.

There are separate lines for Tropical Fresh Water (TF), Fresh Water (F), Tropical Salt Water (T), Summer Salt Water (S), Winter Salt Water (W), and Winter North Atlantic (WNA). The heaviest loads can be carried by ships headed for the tropics, where the sea is calm. The lighter loads can be carried by ships headed for the rough seas of the North Atlantic.

The Plimsoll Lines, were invented by a British merchant and politician, named Samuel Plimsoll. Before he devised these lines, ships were often overloaded and many sailors died at sea. Plimsoll publicized the scandal of these "coffin ships" and in 1876, the British government enforced Plimsoll Lines. The United States eventually followed, and passed the Load Line Act in 1929.

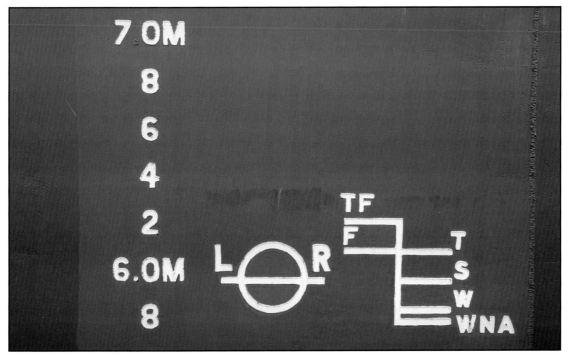

Plimsoll Lines are painted on the sides of merchant ships. These indicate the water levels at which a ship can safely float in different waters.

Earth has many layers, each with a different density. Scientists cannot use scales or other equipment to physically weigh Earth or measure the density of its innermost cores. Instead, they use known formulas and calculations.

CHAPTER FIVE

Weighing without Scales

How could a person determine how much Earth weighs? In 1798, a British scientist named Henry Cavendish was able to figure out how much our planet weighed. Many consider his measurement to be one of the great achievements in the history of science. More than a century earlier, Sir Isaac Newton had explained that every object has gravity. The amount of this gravity depends on the object's mass and a tiny gravitational force. However, the force was too small for Newton to measure. Cavendish set out to measure this force.

He started with two little balls of equal mass. He hung one at each end of a very thin rod that was about 2 meters long. He suspended the rod at its center using wire. Near each end, but not attached to the rod were larger balls. These two large balls, of equal mass, were on opposite sides of the rod. What happened? The small balls and the big ones pulled on each other because of their gravity. The ends of the rod swung around in opposite directions, twisting the wire. Cavendish set a little mirror on the wire and beamed light on to it. As the wire twisted, the beam of light was reflected onto tiny ivory scales. The position of the reflected beam on the scales enabled him to measure the movement of the rod's ends. This gave him a measure of the force between the small and large balls.

Cavendish then tried the experiment with different size balls. The amount of twist varied with different sizes. He found that the twist depended on the distance between the balls, the balls' masses, and an unchanging tiny factor. This unchanging factor was the gravitational force.

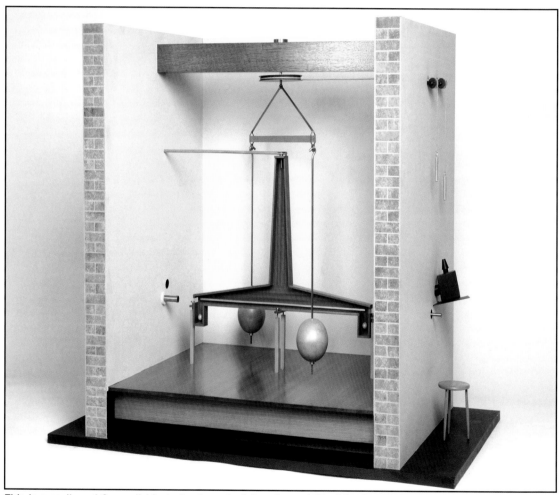

This is a replica of Cavendish's device for calculating the weight of Earth and the gravitational constant. The balance he used is called a torsion balance because it uses the amount of torsion, or twisting force, that results from the attraction between two objects.

EARTH'S DENSITY

Geologists—scientists who study the physical structure and the processes of Earth—use density when exploring the interior of Earth. The planet as a whole must be about 5-1/2 times denser than water. Earth's surface rocks are only 2.8 times the density of water, so scientists believe that parts of Earth must be much more dense. Earth's density steadily increases the deeper one goes. At a depth of 1,800 miles, Earth has a liquid core that is denser than the surface rocks.

This force is a constant throughout the universe but it is extremely small. On two 1-pound balls that are 1 foot apart, the constant is equivalent to a force of 1/2 billionth of an ounce.

Since he knew the measurement of the tiny gravitational force, Cavendish could calculate Earth's weight. Since the gravitational force is so tiny, the mass of Earth had to be enormous for Earth's gravity to make a 1-pound mass weigh one pound. Working backward from the tiny gravitational force, he calculated the enormous weight of Earth. In fact, Earth's weight is about 6,595,000,000,000,000,000,000 tons. In words, that is six thousand five hundred, ninety-five billion trillion tons. Knowing the weight of Earth, and knowing its size, the planet's density can be worked out. Earth's average density is about 5-1/2 times the density of water.

WEIGHING ATOMS

Atoms are the building blocks of all matter. The smallest piece of any chemical element that still has the characteristics of that element is an atom. For example, oxygen atoms display the same chemical properties or characteristics that the element oxygen has. Atoms are far too small to be viewed with an ordinary microscope that uses light, so you cannot see them. Atoms are also too light to weigh on a scale. So how could anyone possibly weigh an atom?

British scientist F. W. Aston found a way in 1919. He used magnetism to weigh atoms. In doing this, he invented the first device that measures atomic mass, called the **mass spectrometer**. Today the mass spectrometer is used by chemists and other scientists.

Aston started with neon gas in a glass flask. (Neon is a type of gas that glows when an electric

Aston's first mass spectrograph—now called a spectrometer—was created around 1919.

THE ATOM

Atoms are made up of smaller particles. However, unlike atoms, these particles do not have the characteristics or properties of a specific element. These particles are called **protons**, **electrons**, and **neutrons**. Protons are positively charged particles and they are located inside the atom's **nucleus**, or center. Electrons are negatively charged particles and travel around the nucleus. Neutrons are neutral and have no charge. An atom's neutrons are located in the nucleus. The numbers of protons, electrons, and neutrons help to determine an atom's properties. For example, a carbon atom has six electrons, while a silver atom has forty-seven. Because of the way they are made up, carbon atoms and silver atoms behave in different ways.

A computer illustration shows the different parts of an atom. Protons and neutrons (yellow and blue) are in the atom's nucleus. Electrons (white) orbit around the nucleus in different layers or shells.

current is passed through it.) Inside each end of the flask was a metal plate. He connected the plates to a battery. The battery had two **terminals**—one was a negative terminal and the other one was a positive terminal. Each plate in the flask was attached to one of the terminals. This gave one plate a positive charge, and the other a negative charge. An electric current then traveled through the gas from one plate to the other. In doing so, it stripped negatively charged electrons off the atoms, leaving the atoms with a positive electric charge.

The positively charged atoms were attracted to the negative plate and moved toward it. Aston had drilled a hole in this plate, so charged atoms passed through the hole into a glass tunnel. Around the tunnel Aston had placed a semicircular electromagnet.

The magnet bent the stream of positively charged atoms, which then hit a special coating at the end of the tube. The coating registered the impact of the atoms as lines of light. To Aston's astonishment, there were two lines of light on the coating. Some of the atoms had been bent more than others. This meant that some were heavier than the others.

NEUTRONS AND ISOTOPES

Usually, the neutrons in an atom weigh the same amount as an atom's protons. But isotopes of a particular element have the same number of protons and electrons, but a different number of neutrons. These extra (or fewer) neutrons are why isotopes have different weights.

Chemists already knew that neon atoms were about twenty times heavier than hydrogen atoms. However, until Aston did his experiments, nobody knew that neon atoms came in two sizes. He found that 90 percent of neon was twenty times heavier than hydrogen. The remaining 10 percent of the neon weighed more. Both sizes of neon atoms had the same chemistry, but weighed different amounts. These atoms of the same element but with different weights were named isotopes.

Following Aston's pioneering work, scientists now know that many elements have two or more isotopes. Different isotopes can have special uses. For example, sometimes isotopes of certain elements have properties that make them useful in medical research. In nuclear power generation, which splits atoms to create energy, the **radioactive** isotope uranium 135 is used to enrich the heavier uranium 138, which is not radioactive. Together, they create enough radioactivity to heat water, which is turned to the steam that is used to drive electricity generators.

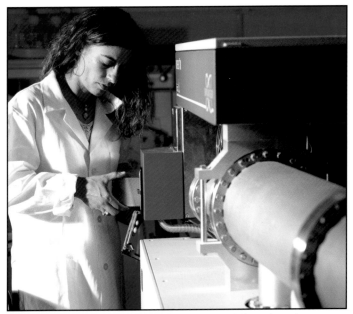

A researcher uses a mass spectrometer to weigh and analyze an object's chemical makeup.

Mass spectrometers are used for more than determining isotopes. Scientists today use the machines to analyze chemicals and other substances. The mass spectrometer can tell them the weights of the different chemicals that make up the substance. They can usually identify the chemicals by these weights. This is especially useful in instances in which a scientist has a mystery substance that he or she cannot identify.

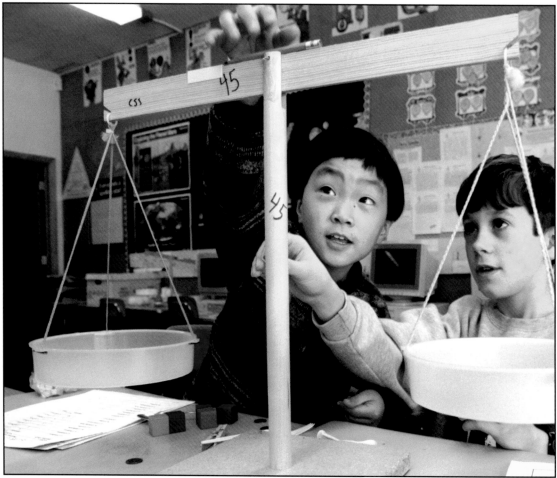

Determining weights is not just for scientists—people of all ages can use formulas and weighing equipment to learn more about weight.

THE IMPORTANCE OF WEIGHT

Knowing about weight is essential for everyday life. We use weight to learn more about our own bodies. When grocery shopping, weighing scales tells us how much food we are buying. Our pharmacists can give us the right amount of medication because of their special weighing scales.

Engineers who build bridges, roads, or buildings have to calculate the weight of structures. They must use weight measurements to figure out how much weight a structure can safely support. Tunnel builders must know the weight of the riverbed above the tunnel so that they can make the tunnel strong enough to be safe.

Geologists investigate density in different parts of Earth. This will help them search for geological fault lines that may cause earthquakes, or find deposits that may contain oil.

The work of scientists and engineers always builds on the knowledge of earlier science pioneers. Our knowledge of weight goes back over many centuries, and has become greater and greater with time. Today, we can use our knowledge of atomic weights to create new life-saving drugs. By understanding how weight is defined by gravity, we can design space vehicles to explore other planets in our solar system. As our knowledge about measurements grows, the possibilities for technology and other advancements become limitless.

GLOSSARY

atoms—Small particles that are the building blocks of all matter.

buoyancy—The ability of an object to float in a liquid.

circumference—The measured distance around the outside of a circle or sphere.

density—A measurement of how heavy an object is in terms of its volume. It is measured in units of weight per volume (weight/volume).

displacement—When an object takes the place of another. Used as a method for determining an object's volume.

electromagnet—A magnet that works when an electric current runs through it.

electrons—Negatively charged particles that orbit the nucleus of an atom.

gravity—The force that pulls things toward one another, causing objects to have weight.

horizontal—Straight across, like the horizon.

isotopes—Different forms of the same element that have different numbers of neutrons.

lever—A bar or rod used to lift things.

libra—A standard weight used by the Ancient Romans. It is equal to about 3/4 of a present-day pound.

mass—The amount of matter in an object.

mass spectrometer—A device used to identify substances by determining the different isotopes' masses.

mina—A standard weight used by the Ancient Babylonians. Its weight equaled the weight of 50 shekels, which is about 1 pound today.

neutrons—Particles located in an atom's nucleus; they are neither negatively nor positively charged.

nucleus—The center of an atom that holds protons and neutrons.

pivot—In a balance, the central part that supports the balance.

protons—Positively charged particles located in an atom's nucleus.

radioactive—To give off invisible rays of energy when atoms split apart.

sea level—The level of the ocean's surface. It is used to measure the depths of the oceans and land elevation or altitude.

shekel—A standard weight first used by the Ancient Babylonians, it was equal to about 1/4 of an ounce today. It is also a unit of money in Israel.

talent—A standard weight first used by the Ancient Babylonians, it was equal to the weight of 60 minas, or 60 pounds.

terminals—In batteries, the places where an electric current leaves or enters.

uncia—A weight used by the Romans, which was 1/16 the weight of a libra.

volume—The amount of space an object occupies.

FIND OUT MORE

BOOKS

Farndon, John. *Gravity, Weight, and Balance.* Tarrytown, NY: Benchmark Books, 2002.

Gardner, Robert. *Heavy-Duty Science Projects with Weight: How Much Does It Weigh?* Berkeley Heights, NJ: Enslow Publishers, 2003.

Nardo, Don. *Gravity.* San Diego, CA: KidHaven Press, 2003.

WEB SITES

GRACE: Gravity Recovery and Climate Experiment (NASA)
http://www.csr.utexas.edu/grace

ScienceKids: Gravity
http://www.cs.dartmouth.edu/farid/sciencekids/gravity.html

METRIC CONVERSIONS

UNITS OF WEIGHT

CUSTOMARY OR TRADITIONAL
1 pound = 12 ounces
1 U.S. hundredweight = 100 pounds
1 U.S. ton = 20 hundredweights

METRIC
1 kilogram = 1,000 grams
1 metric tonne = 1,000 kilograms

1 kilogram = 2.2 pounds

To convert customary units to metric units you can do the following:

metric tonne = U.S. ton x 0.907
kilogram = U.S. hundredweight x 45.36
kilogram = pound x 0.4536
gram = ounce x 0.035

To convert metric units to customary units you can do the following:

U.S. ton = tonne x 1.10
U.S. hundredweight = kilograms x 0.022
pound = kilograms x 2.2
ounce = grams x 28.35

Answer to question on page 32:

The different objects will float at different levels because of density. For example, if an object is more dense than one of the oils, it will not float above the oil

INDEX

PAGES NUMBERS FOR ILLUSTRATIONS ARE IN **BOLDFACE**

ABOUT THE AUTHOR

Navin Sullivan has an M.A. in science from the University of Cambridge. He lives with his wife in London, England, and has dedicated many years to science education. He has edited various science texts, and has written science books for younger readers. Navin Sullivan has also been the CEO of a British educational publisher and Chairman of its Boston subsidiary. His hobbies include playing the piano and chess.